# Arthur Meighen

John English

Fitzhenry & Whiteside Limited

# Contents

English, John, 1945-
  Arthur Meighen

(The Canadians)

Bibliography: p. 64
ISBN 0-88902-242-9 pa.

1. Meighen, Arthur, 1874-1960.   2. Prime ministers — Canada —
Biography.   3. Canada — Politics and government —
1921-
1930.*   I. Series.

FC556.M44355     971.06'13'0924     C77-001401-1
F1034.M46E55

**The Author**

*John English is Assistant Professor of History at the University of
Waterloo. He has written books and articles about 20th century Canadian history and politics, including a biography of Robert Borden.*

©1977 Fitzhenry and Whiteside Limited
    150 Lesmill Road,
    Don Mills, Ontario M3B 2T5

*Printed and bound in Canada.*

*ISBN 0-88902-242-9*

# Arthur Meighen Chapter 1

The town lies in the valley that follows the river. Those
who came first to St. Mary's, Upper Canada, were British, and they called the river the Thames. Like nearly all
the small communities in mid-nineteenth century south-
western Ontario, St. Mary's was nurtured by the river.
Both the sawmill and the gristmill depended upon the
power of the water's flow, and the community in turn
needed the mills to survive and prosper. When a young
Irishman, Gordon Meighen, came to St. Mary's in 1843,
the small community's survival was still in doubt. His
work as the village's first schoolmaster would remove
some of that doubt. In Gordon Meighen's one-room
school, made of limestone, like so many of the structures
of the area, the young of St. Mary's learned those tools
which enabled them to measure logs and land, and also
became aware of the wider world beyond their protected
valley. In those days students learned not only facts but
also the values of their community. These values were
unmistakably British and Protestant, sometimes even
Puritan: hard work, respect for authority and tradition,
and not least, individualism.

An industrious individualist himself, Gordon
Meighen knew that a schoolmaster's salary could barely

*The North Ward, St. Mary's,
Ontario, c. 1900*

*The Canada Company's coat of arms. How did the Company encourage settlement and development?*

sustain a family. Besides, he had always wanted a farm and so he obtained one from the Canada Company which developed the area. The farm meant much work. The land had not been cleared; no house had been built. With Gordon's early death in 1859, these tasks fell upon his eldest son, Joseph, and he, together with his six children, made the farm both a home and a source of a comfortable income. The family's success was taken as an affirmation of those solid values which Gordon Meighen had passed to his children and which Joseph sought to pass to his. The second of Joseph's children, Arthur, believed this most devoutly, and throughout a life which took him far beyond the family farm, Arthur showed the strength of his belief.

Arthur Meighen — his thrifty Presbyterian parents gave him no middle name — was born in 1874. Queen Victoria had already reigned for thirty-seven years and had emerged from the seclusion following her husband's death to stamp her imprint upon the age. Her Canadian subjects were as much influenced by the spirit of the Victorian age as were the British themselves, and nowhere was this so true as in Meighen's southern Ontario. The Meighens shared the Victorian belief in progress, a belief that man was capable of and was undergoing both material and moral improvement.

*What qualities do we associate with the Victorian age?*

*Celebrations for Queen Victoria's Diamond Jubilee in 1897, London*

Reform would spread those benefits enjoyed in past ages by only a few to the many. But reform did not mean revolution: church, family, and school — the established institutions — would provide the foundation for change and would be strengthened by it. Such was the outlook of Joseph Meighen and his children.

Arthur's mother believed that her son's contribution to society could best be made through teaching. This required, however, that the Meighens leave the farm for a home closer to the village, because rural education at that time offered little more than the basics necessary for life on the land. Arthur therefore attended St. Mary's Collegiate where "academic" subjects were taught and apparently taught very well. His classmates may have thought him a drudge. He was awkward on the playing field, shy with all but a few, and outstanding in his school work. He might have been almost unnoticed except for one special talent — debating. What a transformation occurred when Arthur stood before an audience defending some cause of the day! Suddenly, the reserved, spare young man seemed to tower; his strong, sure voice bursting forth in convincing argument while his hands, in rhythm with the speech, seemed to conduct his audience. He scored his points not through appeals to emotion but rather through the careful and steady accumulation of reasoned arguments for his point of view. That these arguments were presented in rich, even elegant English prose made them all the more convincing.

Arthur's speeches showed the coherence and rationality of a mathematical mind, and it is not surprising that "Math." was his best subject. When he had to decide what field he would enter at the University of Toronto, he chose mathematics. Entering the University in 1892, he joined a group of students who would achieve great eminence in the future. One of them would become a British cabinet minister, another a prime minister of Canada. The latter, William Lyon Mackenzie King, already revealed the skills and personality which would carry him so far. Unlike Meighen, the sociable, ambitious and talented King stood out among his classmates. When King led a student strike against the firing of a popular professor, Meighen quietly followed. While King revelled in his leadership role and in this challenge to authority, Meighen worried about it. Upon graduation, the two future prime ministers went markedly different ways. King, already a public figure in Toronto, went on to the University of Chicago and Harvard; Meighen left quietly, deciding that he would seek his first job in a small country store near his home in St. Mary's.

This was definitely an odd choice for a young man with a first class degree in mathematics. Within a few weeks, Meighen realized his mistake. Yielding to his mother's wishes, he entered the teacher training programme at the provincial College of Education. Again, he made a bad choice.

His initial teaching experience was most discouraging. In his first teaching position in a small Ontario town, Meighen scolded and sent home a student who was (unfortunately for him) the daughter of the school board chairman. Soon the chairman, confident of his authority, stormed into Meighen's classroom and denounced the new teacher. Meighen would not budge. Taking the matter before the entire board of education, he demanded that the chairman should resign; otherwise he would.

After winning an initial vote, Meighen lost when the full board voted. True to his promise, he resigned, and hoped it would be the end of his teaching career.

The incident reveals many persistent traits in Meighen's character: his integrity, his quick temper when threatened, and his unwillingness to bend to fit the mood and the manner of the times. Personal success and circumstances were not as important to him as the defence of what he believed was right. These were, of course, admirable qualities, but they were not those of the average man. The very strength of Meighen's convictions could become his greatest weakness if he failed to appreciate and, indeed, respect the different beliefs of other people. Rigidity might win respect but seldom would it capture popularity. Only those who knew Meighen best came to realize that his stern, cold public manner actually masked a generous, humane nature.

Meighen took his defeat at the hands of the school board very hard. When his St. Mary's teaching career ended so abruptly, he decided to become a part of that exciting national adventure, the opening of the Canadian West.

# Chapter 2 Lawyer and Politician

Some went west dreaming of gold; others, more reasonably, thought of wheat; Arthur Meighen's hopes rested upon — of all things — dried fruit. It seemed so simple. Using his own money and some from friends, he bought a half-interest in a patent on a dried fruit cleaning machine. He took the machine with him to Winnipeg, where he planned to satisfy what he sensed was a western craving for dried fruit. Unfortunately, the rough-edged Westerners craved that delicacy in insufficient quantity. Meighen lost his money, and even worse, he had to return to teaching to repay his debts. He had intended to become a lawyer, but because of the dried fruit failure, he had to wait over a year before he could afford to begin his training in law.

Manitoba had no law school in 1900. Instead of formal training, prospective lawyers had to serve a period of apprenticeship (articling) with members of the province's bar. Meighen did this at several firms, completing his articles in the prosperous, medium-sized town of Portage la Prairie. It was a wise choice. Perhaps because Portage la Prairie was, like St. Mary's, small enough to enable newcomers to form acquaintances quickly, he made his way easily. As always, he worked hard, acquired close friends, won respect, and soon was recognized as a very talented and honourable young man.

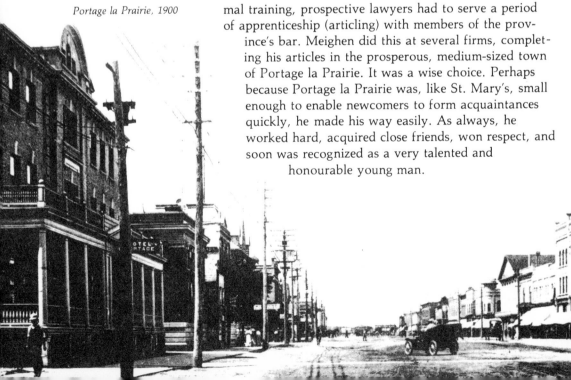

*Portage la Prairie, 1900*

In June of 1904 Meighen married a school teacher named Isabel Cox. Isabel taught in Birtle, Manitoba, 240 km away, but the couple managed to carry on a courtship for two years before they decided to marry. Their first child, Theodore Roosevelt O'Neil, was born in the autumn of 1905. Another son, Max, was born in 1908, and a daughter, Lilian, in 1910.

*The Meighens' first son was named after United States President Theodore Roosevelt, who held office from 1901 to 1908.*

While his life and work thrived in Portage la Prairie, Meighen's interests broadened, and he began to look beyond the narrow boundaries of the town. Politics — that is, Conservative politics — fascinated him; and when the chance for the Conservative nomination for the federal constituency of Portage la Prairie came, he quickly grasped it. To the surprise of everyone, including himself, he won the election against the incumbent Liberal in the general election of 1908. Even more impressive was the fact that his victory came as the national Conservative Party went down to their fourth consecutive defeat at the hands of Sir Wilfrid Laurier's Liberals. Obviously Meighen was a man to watch.

Like so many others before and after him, the young Member from Portage was intimidated at first by the House of Commons. There were so many rules to learn, traditions to follow, and so many enemies searching for weaknesses in new members. By the end of his second session, however, Meighen had mastered the treacherous parliamentary path, and his performances in debate were noted for their eloquent and concise presentation of the Conservative case. The skills he had learned and the

*Laurier addressing the House of Commons at the Victoria Museum. Why was the House not sitting in the Parliament buildings when this picture was taken?*

talents he had revealed at St. Mary's Collegiate and in Manitoba's courts served him well in Ottawa. He would eventually be ranked with Blake and Cartwright, Laurier and Diefenbaker, as a parliamentarian who dominated the Commons in his time. Some even say that, in strength of presentation and rational argument, Meighen was the greatest of all. He had a precious gift; but, alas, it was not one which he always used to best effect. Robert Borden, Meighen's leader and one who lacked Meighen's oratorical talents, later commented that Meighen's greatest talent could often be his greatest defect. Rather than scattering his opponents with a few well-placed shots, he hunted them down mercilessly, sending forth persistent volleys of sarcastic wit to destroy all his enemies. The technique rouses one's friends, but it does not win over enemies, something one must do in politics. This Meighen never learned.

These problems, however, were not apparent in the early parliamentary years when he began to make his mark upon Canadian politics. His major concern then was merely to stay in the Commons. This task did not seem easy in the election of 1911. The Conservatives opposed reciprocity (a form of free trade with the United States), which was a popular cause in the Canadian West. Nevertheless, Meighen campaigned hard, shaking hands until he could no more, and travelling by buggy to the remote corners of his Portage riding. When asked what was wrong with reciprocity, his answer was characteristically straightforward: it would undermine Canada's national economic unity and assure American dominance over Canada's economy. Meighen could not accept this as a possibility; neither could his constituency nor the majority of his countrymen. Meighen's majority tripled, and for the first time in fifteen years, the Conservatives won a general election. A grander triumph could not be imagined.

*The people of Canada rejected reciprocity in 1911. To what extent could the same arguments be used today with regard to Canadian-American trade?*

The lustre of the victory may have been somewhat tarnished for Meighen when Prime Minister Borden did not choose him for a cabinet post, but did appoint other Manitobans. One of these Manitoba appointees was Meighen's personal rival, Robert Rogers, "the Hon. Bob," a high-living backroom politician whose greatest delight came in plucking the plums of patronage.

Borden's inexperienced but determined government

*Robert Borden, in London for
a meeting of the Imperial
Defence Committee in 1912*

soon ran into trouble over its naval bill, which proposed
to contribute money to Britain for the defence of Britain's and, in their eyes, Canada's Empire. In defending
this policy, the Conservative cabinet had no match for
the sharp eloquence and knowledge of parliamentary
rules displayed on the Liberal front bench. Day after
day, month after month, the Commons debate continued. Frustration grew and tempers flared; the
Conservatives began to seek some method by which they
could silence the Opposition. Meighen, already a shrewd
master of Parliament's rules, urged Borden to introduce
closure, a device used in the British Parliament to end          *What is closure?*
debates which would otherwise be interminable. Even-
tually Borden accepted Meighen's advice, to the Liberals'
great dismay and astonishment. The victory, however,

*Today the Senate rarely refuses to approve bills passed by the Commons. Why?*

was only temporary: the Liberal-dominated Senate, outraged by the gagging of their colleagues in the Commons, refused to approve the naval bill. On these shoals of bitterness, Canada's fledgling navy was scuttled.

As a result of the closure debate, Meighen won the lasting suspicion of the Grits, as he called the Liberals, but he also commanded increased respect from Conservatives. Such an eloquent speaker with such an inventive mind surely deserved a higher post. Borden agreed, and in June 1913, he appointed Meighen Solicitor General. As expected, Meighen immediately devoted his considerable energy and ability to his new position. Because of this preoccupation, he may have had less time to follow events in Europe, which would soon affect his career and his nation more than anything the Canadian government alone was deciding. But when the first guns were fired in August 1914, Meighen was not the only one surprised at how serious the European situation had become. Indeed, few Canadians realized how great the impact of war would be.

*Meighen in 1912*

# The Great War Chapter 3

While Sam Hughes, Borden's boisterous and incredible
Minister of Militia, rallied "his boys," as he called
Canada's infant army, to the British cause, Meighen
prepared the legal foundations upon which the Canadian
war effort would rest.

Hughes revelled in war, its action, excitement and
combat; Meighen, like most Canadians, loathed war and
the death and destruction it caused. This does not mean
that he believed that Canada should not fight. In 1914,
there seemed no choice; Kaiser Wilhelm's Germany was
seen as a malignant cancer upon the larger Western
civilization of which Canada was a part. Although this
civilization was already falling from the heights of the
triumphant Victorian era, it still seemed worth defending.

For the young Manitoba politician of modest up-
bringing, the war was an awful but necessary defence of
those values which he cherished. He even considered
enlisting; after all, forty-one was not too old for the
trenches, where he believed he could best make a state-
ment of what the war meant to him. But Borden would
not hear of it; Meighen had become too valuable to him
and to the nation. Thus, rather than join the Canadian
Expeditionary Force in 1915, he became a full-fledged
member of the cabinet.

Borden pushed Meighen into a chaotic political situation. Laurier's Liberals had promised, when the war
began, to raise no objections to government policy so
long as there was danger at the front. That promise was
not kept. As justification for their attacks on the government, the Liberals pointed to widespread scandal and in-
efficiency in the Conservative management of the war.
Unfortunately there was much truth in the charge. The
Canadian state was not yet strong enough to carry the
burden of such a large-scale war. The civil service was
very small and could not watch over the new activities
which the government assumed in wartime. Never before
had the federal government been asked to do so much,
and naturally, it made many mistakes. The worst abuses
occurred within Sam Hughes' Militia Department where

*General Sir Sam Hughes. To what extent was Hughes responsible for the tension between French and English Canadians in World War I?*

Hughes gave political cronies lucrative war contracts. Sir Sam often seemed more concerned about his own glory than his nation's. This enraged the Liberals; it also disturbed Meighen and Borden, but not until mid-1916 did Hughes depart from the cabinet.

Hughes' firing signalled a new attitude towards the war. Canadians and their government realized that the war was a severe test of the nation's political and economic system. Political difficulties arose from Canadians' varying perceptions of the war. To most English Canadians, it was Canada's war, a battle to uphold those traditions and values which Canadians held dear. It was, in the words of Borden, a fight to the last man and to the last dollar. To most French Canadians, however, World War I was a British war: Canadian involvement was legitimate recognition of the protection which Britain had given to Canada in the past, but this involvement in a British war should never mean the exhaustion of Canada or the end of her national unity. Meighen neither agreed with nor understood the French-Canadian outlook, and in 1916 and 1917 he became recognized as one of the most effective spokesmen for the Anglophone viewpoint. This had the unfortunate result of making him an antagonist in the eyes of French Canadians.

Meighen also played a leading part at this time in the solution of Canada's major economic problem, her

*C.P.R. Engine No. 47 at
Donald, B.C., c. 1910*

bankrupt railways. Before the war, railways were often
built not so much to carry passengers as to cover political debts. When the country was booming, the wealthier
sections of the railways could maintain the poorer ones,
but the war ended that happy situation for nearly all the
railways, except the Canadian Pacific. As so often hap-
pens, the failure of private enterprise brought the intervention of government. Faced with a desperate situation,
the government nationalized the Canadian Northern
Railway in 1917 at great political cost to itself and great
financial cost to future generations. In theory Meighen,
as the Solicitor General, had nothing to do with railways, but the war had weakened the government, leaving few effective parliamentary fighters. When the
Liberals began to attack the government on their nationalization plan, the government's best defender naturally
moved to the forefront of the debate.

*What are the responsibilities
of the Solicitor General?*

Meighen more than met the Liberals' challenge, but
he paid a heavy price: the Montreal railway and banking
interests associated with the CPR never forgave him for
his eloquence at this time. These businessmen saw nationalization as a threat to the CPR. It was at any rate a
threat to their personal interests, since they would not
have the influence to which they were accustomed if the
railroad were under government control. The *Montreal
Star* and the *Gazette*, both organs for the CPR interests,

continued to harass Meighen throughout his political career, often refusing him support even though they were traditional backers of the Conservative party.

The Anglo-Canadian businessmen of Montreal were important to a politician, but not as important as the businessmen thought they were. The French Canadians were of much more significance in the long run, and during the course of the war Borden and his ministers increasingly offended French Canada. The government reflected the opinion of the English-Canadian part of the nation which was growing more suspicious and hostile towards French Canada. The failure of French Canadians to enlist in what their countrymen regarded as satisfactory numbers was the major source of tension.

French Canadians answered the charges by pointing to the English-Canadian domination of the war effort: the appointment of a Protestant war minister to recruit French-Canadian Catholics, the refusal to permit French Canadians to serve under French-Canadian command, and most of all, Ontario's limitations on the teaching of French in that province. To be fair, there was little that the federal government could do about the provincial government's action, but it should not have appeared as indifferent as it did.

The French-Canadian nationalist Henri Bourassa emerged as the most outspoken leader of the opposition to Ontario's action. In his newspaper *Le Devoir* and on public platforms, he denounced the restrictions on French Canadians in Ontario. In December 1915, he claimed "there are 200 000 French Canadians today living under worse oppression in Ontario than the people of Alsace-Lorraine under the iron heel of Prussia." Why fight Prussia in Europe when Prussianism existed at home? The arguments had an effect, and by late 1916, French Canadians were refusing to fight in the British war. In the spring of 1917, Borden's government, under pressure from the English-Canadian majority, said they must. The government introduced conscription — compulsory military service — which only a year earlier Borden had promised would never be introduced.

Meighen, as the best spokesman for the Military Service Act, was a prime target of the wrath which Borden's government brought on itself. It must be admitted that Meighen's reply to Laurier's attack upon conscription

*Henri Bourassa*

had little of the evasiveness and delicacy which normally mark debates on such sensitive subjects. There was, Meighen declared in the Commons, "a backward and a forward portion of the population of every country that ever existed in the world." He continued: "If we can only produce union by walking at the speed of and abreast with the backward portion of the Canadian people, then I do not want union in Canada; I am rather ready to face disorder and dissension." The words stung; they were not forgotten.

A few months later in this turbulent political year, Meighen introduced the controversial Wartime Elections Bill. It withdrew the right to vote from many thousands of "enemy aliens" — Canadians who were under suspicion because of their German origin. The brashness of this act is astonishing in retrospect; citizens of Canada who had voted in several elections in the past and who had been loyal were not permitted to exercise their franchise. Meighen claimed that this action, unique in the Western democracies, was necessary because these "enemy aliens" were not liable for military service. War service, Meighen argued, must be the basis for wartime citizenship. The legislation was a shocking breach of Canadian democratic practice. Moreover, the act was unnecessary even in political terms: the "aliens" were not so numerous that their vote would have defeated the conscriptionists in an election. No, the explanation for

*Immigrants from Hamburg, Germany heading west from Quebec, 1911*

*Sir George Foster*

this extraordinary move was fear, fear that "alien" forces within and without the nation were combining to destroy it. The pressure of war explains the emotion — but does not excuse the act.

Meighen's reward for his efforts was the Ministry of the Interior in the Union Government, which was formed in October 1917. This government brought together Liberals and Conservatives committed to conscription. French Canadians regarded this government as a coalition against them, and to a certain extent they were correct. English-Canadian Liberals deserted their French-Canadian leader to join with their Conservative counterparts to enforce conscription. The Unionists made no attempt to present their case in Quebec; elsewhere they spared no effort and used every technique which might assure their triumph in the election. A pre-election speech by Sir George Foster set the unfortunate tone for the campaign: "Every alien enemy sympathizer, every man of alien blood born in an alien country with few exceptions, is with Sir Wilfrid Laurier, and every Hun sympathizer from Berlin to the trenches, from Berlin to the Cameroons, wishes success to Laurier, with his anti-conscriptionist campaign." With such rhetoric ringing in their ears, French Canadians no longer bothered to disguise their opposition to the war and their disgust with Canada's wartime leaders, especially Arthur Meighen.

In December 1917, Union Government faced the electorate and the result was resounding approval. Meighen's majority was multiplied several times in Portage la Prairie, and the Unionists won over one hundred and fifty seats, the largest number of any party in Canadian history to that time. The campaign and the year left memories, however, and perhaps the strongest were those of French Canadians and of the "enemy aliens" of the West. These people would not forget the grave, cold member for Portage describing them as "backward" and in some cases, denying their rights.

For Meighen, 1917 was a year of triumph, vindication of his efforts and hopes. But on that election night as he celebrated his own and his party's victory, the curtain which cloaked the future lay closed. Behind it, the actors who would determine his fate had already taken their places.

vote against the
vernment means:

ou are here
for life

A vote for the
Government means:

Another man
is coming to
take your place

Printed and Published by THE HAYCOCK-CABLE CO., Hasts Street, Camberwell, London, S.E. 5

This Unionist poster was posted at the European front in the 1917 election. Weary Canadian troops responded with votes in support of the government.

# Chapter 4 Unionism After the War

Arthur Meighen in wartime defined his own Conservatism and helped to give definition to his party which, since the death of Sir John A. Macdonald in 1891, had often groped for meaning. Borden himself had once said that there was no real distinction between Canadian Liberals and Conservatives. Nevertheless, the reciprocity election and the war had shown that the prosperous Laurier years had merely hidden and not eliminated the differences between the parties.

Fundamentally, the most important difference concerned the concept of leadership. Meighen believed that leadership was the task of identifying larger national goals and directing Canadians towards them. The leader was not simply a delegate of the electors, one who only reflected and acted upon their wishes. If a section of the nation remained "backward," the leader's duty was to bring that section forward, educating it in the duties of citizenship. In the end, the backward would see the wisdom of such leadership. The history of England and her Empire, which Meighen so cherished, demonstrated the value of such leadership: the common people, whatever their own attitudes, ultimately benefitted from the farsightedness of their rulers. Elizabeth, Pitt, Cromwell and Disraeli were each plagued by doubters, but convinced of their visions, these leaders persisted, assuring the future liberty and prosperity of Englishmen.

Since he felt political direction should come from the wisdom of a few men rather than from the people as a whole, Meighen was an elitist. Nevertheless, he did not favour a traditional, hereditary aristocracy on the British model, as indeed, few Canadian Conservatives did. Meighen was thoroughly Canadian in this belief as in all other matters. However much he admired British precedents, he felt that the North American system improved upon them. Meighen saw here the opportunity for a system where the best people, whatever their origins,

*The artist entitled this drawing of Meighen, "The Helm in Safe Hands."*

could lead in a fashion consistent with the traditions of the nation and its hopes for the future — a sort of aristocracy of ability. Leaders as well as citizens acquired their rights by service, not by birth. In 1917, Meighen had seen this legitimate political argument as a justification for restricting the franchise of some and ignoring the objections of many others. His consistency is undeniable, but his political wisdom is not. Not for the last time, Meighen took his argument too far for many Canadians to follow.

His effective defence of difficult positions impressed many of his Conservative colleagues, but admittedly troubled others. His old political antagonist, Bob Rogers, who was as ready to bend a principle as to give a friend a job, found Meighen too inflexible, too willing to yield valuable votes when a principle was the only price. Nor did the Liberal Unionists who joined the government in 1917 much like Meighen. To them, he was too "Tory," too staunch a defender of the Conservative past. Yet even his enemies granted him his great ability, and it

*Politicians often must choose between principle and expediency. How do you think the choice should be made?*

was in recognition of this ability that he was chosen to accompany Borden on his 1918 journey to England to discuss the war and the future. This was Meighen's first visit to Britain, and it confirmed for him how important it was for Canada to remain British. It was a pleasant journey, although Meighen's work in London — the negotiations for the nationalization of the Grand Trunk Railway — was quite difficult. Even greater burdens would fall on him when he returned.

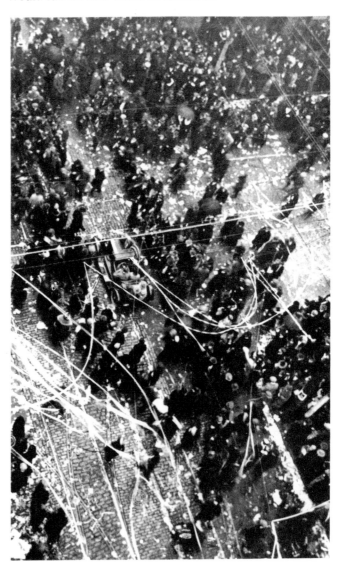

*Victory celebrations in Toronto, 1918*

The Allied victory of November 1918 brought cele-
bration, but also confusion and exhaustion. The Unionist
triumph in the 1917 election had been like a dose of
adrenalin injected into the tired body of Borden's government. Now, less than a year later, its rejuvenating
effect had disappeared. Borden was no longer very inter-
ested in domestic affairs, preferring to deal with what he
thought were the more important subjects being dis-
cussed at the Peace Conference in Paris. The rest of the
cabinet had other problems. Sir Thomas White, the
Finance Minister, was suffering from nervous exhaustion; Sir George Foster was, in Borden's words, next to
useless; and Bob Rogers, now outside the cabinet, was
stirring up trouble among restless Conservative backbenchers. The Liberal infusion in 1917 had provided some
able ministers such as Calder and Mewburn, but with
the war's end, the political future of these former
Liberals was uncertain.

Meighen, by contrast, stood out among the ministers
in vigour, ability and unquestioned loyalty. At times he
acted as the minister for three or four departments; in
the Commons, he parried the Opposition thrusts. With
the death of Laurier in early 1919, Meighen's dominance
of the House became even clearer. However, beyond the
House his footing was less sure and the terrain less
friendly.

After the war, Canada entered a state of economic
and social turmoil. During the war, the vast appetite of
the military had spurred the expansion of Canadian in-
dustry. Those Canadians who stayed at home, whether
workers or farmers, owners or managers, reaped the
financial benefits of this artificial demand. They had
become accustomed to wartime levels of production and
income and the returning soldiers understandably expected to participate in the prosperity too. But these
hopes were unreasonable and could not be fulfilled. In
some cases, wages actually fell. Much of the discontent
caused by economic distress and disappointment was
channelled into the organization of labour unions, which
grew over 250 percent in membership between 1915 and
1919. As their membership grew, the unions became increasingly vocal and militant, demanding new rights and
a place in the Canadian political and social system.

Neither St. Mary's nor Portage la Prairie had taught

*Robert Rogers*

*The end of World War I
brought unrest in many of the
countries that had been fighting. What forms did this
unrest take in countries other
than Canada?*

An airplane factory during the War

Members of the Western Federation of Miners on strike in South Porcupine, Ontario, c. 1915

Meighen much about unions, but these small towns had
given him a profound respect for individualism and sta-
bility. While he was not in fact opposed to the labour
movement's long term goals, he had little patience with
the increasing militancy of labour leaders. Was not his
own career testimony to the openness of Canadian
democracy and to the opportunities available to all
Canadians, regardless of origin, for achieving even the
highest offices? Could not others do the same? With
such an attitude, it is hardly surprising that Meighen
reacted with fear and anger to the radical speeches of
labour leaders after the war.

Ordinarily Meighen would not have been the man to
mediate a strike, but 1919 was in no sense ordinary.
When thousands of workers took to the streets of Winnipeg in a general strike, he recalled the turmoil in St.
Petersburg in 1917, and imagined a similar revolutionary
result in Winnipeg. With Labour Minister Gideon
Robertson, who was a former labour official, Meighen
set out for Winnipeg to determine the strike's causes and
ensure its end. When they arrived, Meighen met many
of his Winnipeg friends at the station. He was shocked
by what they told him. These people, he later recalled,
"were quite certain that what was about to take place in
the Capitol was nothing less than a revolution..." What
he saw — a city paralysed — seemed to confirm these
impressions.

*Was revolution a real possibil-
ity in Winnipeg in 1919? Do
you think the government
handled the strike well?*

Meighen and Robertson immediately ordered striking
federal employees back to work. Refusal to return would
mean the loss of one's job. Yet the strike continued even
when the government strengthened the Criminal Code
specifically to crush it. Moreover, it began to spread as
workers throughout Canada walked off their jobs to
express sympathy with their Winnipeg colleagues. The
government had to respond. Mounted Police moved into
Winnipeg and a confrontation seemed inevitable. On the
first day of summer, the strikers and Mounties clashed.
One person died, and many more were injured. "Bloody
Saturday" ended the strike but not the conditions which
had caused it.

The strikers' anger remained and so did Meighen's.
Events in the remainder of 1919 and in 1920 failed to
calm him. Perhaps what upset him most was neither the
strikers nor Canadian farmers who were declaring their

independence from the traditional Canadian party system, but rather the Liberals' choice of his old classmate, Mackenzie King, as Laurier's successor. Meighen had disliked King ever since their first encounter in the University of Toronto strike long ago. He would quickly come to loathe King, who had a tendency to treat Tories as something unclean and un-Christian. But Meighen's view of King blinded him to King's political skills. He constantly underestimated his pudgy, long-winded opponent, believing that King's appearance was an accurate reflection of reality. It was not.

There was opposition to the strike as well as support. The picture shows a group of Great War Veterans preparing to march on the Legislature to demonstrate their opposition.

Mounties charge down Main Street in Winnipeg on "Bloody Saturday"

A cartoon of King by Les Callan

# Chapter 5 Prime Minister

Prime Minister Borden was sick. His fragile nerves were frayed beyond repair, and doctors at the time could prescribe little but extended rest. But how could a prime minister of a nation in crisis permit himself such a luxury? Obviously he could not and a few days before Christmas 1919, Borden announced that he must resign his office. His cabinet, however, would not hear of it. As so often occurs in a parliamentary system, the cabinet cannot imagine itself continuing without its leader. Only Meighen disagreed: if Borden wanted to go, then he should be permitted to take his well-deserved leave. The political world would not collapse without him.

Nevertheless, Borden heeded the majority's wishes and stayed under an extraordinary arrangement whereby he remained Prime Minister of Canada but would not carry out the functions of the office. Instead, it was planned that he would regain his health in the southern sun and return a year later to re-assume his duties with new strength. The whole idea was absurd. Meighen knew it immediately; others, including Borden, soon agreed. On Dominion Day 1920, Borden finally resigned; a week later Arthur Meighen was chosen as his successor.

Meighen had not been Borden's or the cabinet's first choice: they favoured Sir Thomas White, a conciliator by nature who had been a Liberal until 1911. Communication between Liberal and Conservative Unionists had almost broken down, but Sir Thomas had ties with both groups. He seemed to have a good chance of holding Unionist government together. However, he would not accept the prime ministership and the Conservative caucus would not accept him. Meighen, the favourite of the Conservative backbenchers was then chosen as leader and at the age of forty-five, became the youngest Prime Minister of Canada.

Meighen had craved his new position, but the majesty of his office changed him not at all. He continued to walk to work from his modest home, usually wearing

*A congenial meeting across political lines, about 1912. From left to right: Sir Thomas White, Sir Robert Borden, Sir Wilfrid Laurier, Sir George Foster.*

the threadbare suits which were his mark. His friends from Portage still addressed him as Arthur and did not hesitate to give him advice. To his increasingly demanding father, Meighen was still a dutiful son, giving him the money he expected from his illustrious offspring and paying the older man respectful visits despite a demanding schedule. This was not false modesty or pretended loyalty: Meighen wanted to be remembered not for his style but for his deeds.

Unfortunately, fate was not sympathetic to Meighen's wish. The Borden legacy was a discouraging one. In the brief time remaining before the government had to call an election, Meighen could do little more than assure a decent burial for Union Government. Even that was difficult when some of the fathers of Unionism, like Thomas Crerar, now the leader of the farmers' Progressive Party, denied they had supported the coalition.

Still, Meighen could claim some notable accomplishments. The most significant was his success at the Imperial Conference of 1921 in persuading Britain to end its alliance with Japan, an alliance which could have threatened British and Canadian friendship with the United States. Domestically, Meighen made the nationalization of Canada's bankrupt railways all but permanent, to the dismay of many former Tories. He also refused to renounce the reforms carried out by Union Government, although his backbenchers put enormous pressure on him to return the patronage that civil service reforms had taken from them.

Yet while Meighen defended the present against a return to the past when urged by special interests, he himself was influenced by memories of past glory. When seeking a formula to rekindle the fire in Canadian Conservative hearts, Meighen returned to the protective tariff, an issue which had served the Conservatives so well in the days of Sir John A.

Meighen's diagnosis was correct — Canadians did want to return to what they believed had been a purer, simpler and better time — but his remedy was wrong. The tariff did not stir Canadian hearts and souls in 1921, and there would be an unreal character to any election campaign waged on this false issue. Meighen did not appreciate this, and when he called an election for December 1921, he made the tariff the centerpiece of his platform.

Probably the platform and the issue were irrelevant to the outcome of the campaign: the Conservatives were doomed no matter what programme they presented to the people. Canadians were tired of Union Government. They wanted to forget the war, the divisions it had caused, and in some cases the changes it had made. What they wanted instead, however, was quite unclear.

As always, Meighen worked hard in the campaign, but his performance was a brilliant solo without effective accompaniment. Canadians were more impressed by the Liberals' apparent unity. King in his campaign had conveyed a sense of security and reassurance, although he had not made a striking personal impression. On election day, King won 116 seats, the upstart Progressives — 65, and the Conservatives only 50, less than a third of the 1917 Unionist total. To make the defeat a rout, Meighen lost his own seat in Portage. It seemed he might never win it back.

A Progressive had defeated Meighen in Portage la Prairie, and the new party's hold on Portage and on the Canadian West seemed likely to endure. The Progressives represented the West's disillusionment with the two "old" parties and farmers' resentment towards several of Unionism's wartime actions, especially conscription. To many Westerners, the Liberals and the Conservatives

*What were the planks in the Progressive platform? Why were they more successful in provincial elections than in federal politics?*

*"Preparing for the Plunge" in 1921*

alike were the tools of Eastern interests, which controlled
the banks that refused them credit and the railways
that charged them unfair rates.

Unionism had proven itself even less trustworthy
than single-party government. After promising that
farmers' sons, whose labour was so essential at harvest
time, would be exempt from conscription, Union Government had reversed itself. Moreover, the high agricul-
tural prices of wartime (one Westerner even called the
war "a God-send and a blessing" to the West) fell back
with the arrival of the peace. Again the government was
blamed for a natural economic event. The first indica-
tion of the farmers' political power had come in Ontario
when the United Farmers of Ontario, to their own surprise, won the 1919 provincial election. Soon the federal
Progressive Party took form with Thomas Crerar as its
leader. Crerar's party swept the West in 1921 and even
their opponents believed the party's greatest triumphs
lay in the future.

Meighen, understandably depressed, thought of leaving

politics and returning to law with its lucrative income
— but the thought passed quickly. Soon another
seat was found (in Grenville, Ontario) and he prepared
for Parliamentary battle once again. He still had youth
and eloquence in abundance, but most of all, he had a
burning desire to defeat his successor. During the next
four years, Meighen dominated the Commons until King
and his party could no longer rule the land. Ironically,
Meighen's years in opposition may have been his happi-
est; they were not, however, his finest.

*Thomas Crerar*

# The Epic Duel: Chapter 6
## Challenge...

Arthur Meighen could not understand Mackenzie King. "Indeed," Meighen wrote after the 1921 election, "the senseless utterances of this man pass comprehension and it is indeed difficult to understand how he has advanced in spite of them." As time passed, Meighen became more convinced that his opponent was not a gentleman who engaged in political debate on fair terms. King would distort or evade, and if necessary he would lie. There is much truth in Meighen's charges; even King's supporters

*"The Chameleon (species — Mackenziebus Kingbus). A most interesting and accommodating little creature. If your favourite colour is not visible it will be instantly produced upon the slightest provocation."*

have admitted his annoying evasiveness and frequent attempts to reinterpret his actions in order to cast them in a favourable light. But King's strengths were what his supporters saw more often: his intelligence, his private charm and, above all, his astonishing political foresight. Between 1921 and 1926, the two leaders engaged in a classic political duel in which the brilliant, striking Meighen was eventually worn down by King's dogged persistence.

Meighen struck swiftly at the new prime minister, with such effectiveness that some Conservatives thought King might derive some public sympathy from the onslaught. The Progressives, the second largest party, were divided among themselves and Meighen became Leader of the Opposition in name as well as in reality. King was pestered, ridiculed and frustrated; his neck would redden in anger as Meighen spoke, but he usually remained quiet and seated. Meighen taunted King and his colleagues to take him on: "Speak up," he would challenge the Liberals, "don't behave as your ancestors did ten thousand years ago." Small wonder that distrust soon turned to hatred.

Having re-established his dominance over the House of Commons, Meighen began to rebuild his shattered party. The return of the Conservatives to power in Ontario greatly encouraged him, but the efforts of Bob Rogers and the Montreal railway and press tycoons hindered his work in many areas. There were persistent rumours that the Conservatives were about to rebel and install a new leader. For Meighen, that must have been infuriating. At the very moment when all Conservatives should have been united to take advantage of the problems which the Liberals were having in running the country, they were bickering among themselves. Nevertheless, Meighen persisted and the threats to his leadership never amounted to more than rumours. Soon rewards for his efforts came as Conservatives did well in some by-elections and in provincial elections. The most surprising development was that Conservative prospects in Quebec began to brighten.

Those prospects were certainly not vast, because Meighen's very name continued to be almost a profanity to many French Canadians. Nevertheless, some French-Canadian Conservatives had survived the disaster of

1917, and they began to look to E.-L. Patenaude — a Borden minister who had resigned in 1917 over the conscription issue — as an alternative to Liberal domination of Quebec. Patenaude was popular and capable; his main shortcomings, in Meighen's view, were his associations with Montreal railway and banking interests and his insistence upon claiming independence from the national party and its leader. After extensive discussions with Meighen and other Conservatives, Patenaude finally declared his attachment to Conservative principles and his willingness to become the leader of the French-Canadian Conservatives, but also his freedom from Meighen.

*Esioff-Leon Patenaude*

Patenaude's insistence on independence made sense, for Meighen continued to annoy French Canadians, even as Opposition Leader. Meighen never set out deliberately to offend French Canada; it was not a matter of hatred or prejudice. In fact, he tried (although with little success) to learn French himself in order to show his support of bilingualism. Meighen believed Quebec was as much a part of Canada as any other province, and his anger arose precisely because he thought French Canadians were not contributing responsibly to the good of the state which they shared with English Canadians. Such an attitude was bound to offend French Canadians, who could not have been expected to regard themselves as "backward." To make matters worse, Meighen's forthright manner made his views come through clearly and bluntly, without any subtlety which might have made them seem less insulting. A prime example of this

*The Quebec newspaper Le Soleil was not convinced that Patenaude was independent of Meighen. October, 1925*

**SA LIBERTÉ**

"J'ai les mains libres", s'écrie partout l'hon. M. Patenaude

directness, unfortunate in a politician, occurred during the Chanak crisis in 1922.

This crisis grew out of the defeat of the Greeks, who were Britain's allies, by the Turks under Mustafa Kemal (known as Ataturk). Now British troops faced Turkish guns. Would their allies stand by? This question was directed by cable to Canada, but unfortunately, King received the cable only after the British newspapers had announced on their front pages that a request was going out. King was outraged; public disclosure of the request pressured him unfairly to give his support, when he had not even been consulted during the earlier stages of the crisis. He therefore refused to give the British the affirmative answer they wanted. Parliament, he said, would decide when war came. In the meantime, he would make no promises or commitments.

Meighen and most English-Canadian Conservatives were angered by King's refusal to stand by the Mother Country in time of crisis. Borden had worked and Canadian troops had fought for a Canadian voice in imperial policy. Now all they had achieved might be sacrificed to political expediency by Mackenzie King. Meighen was aware of the dangers of speaking out. The West did not want another war, Quebec would not uphold the imperial cause; but the issue was clear and honour required that he take a stand. So in Toronto, the heartland of imperial sentiment in Canada, Meighen proclaimed his position: "Let there be no dispute as to where I stand. When Britain's message came then Canada should have said: 'Ready, aye ready; we stand by you.'"

"Ready, aye ready" — the phrase haunted Meighen and Canadian Conservatism for too many years. As late as 1956 during the Middle East crisis, Lester Pearson hurled the phrase across the Commons at the Conservatives. His implied charge was the same as that made by other Liberals earlier: Conservatives were ready to follow the British blindly into any imperial war. This charge was unfair, but in French Canada and among other Canadians of non-British ancestry, it was devastatingly effective.

The Chanak crisis as well as Patenaude's self-professed independence assured that Meighen would not play much part in the 1925 election campaign in Quebec. In fact, he never once entered the province. That did not

*"The Trafficker in Human Flesh."* October 29, 1925

stop Quebec Liberals from crude personal attacks on
him. *Le Soleil*, the Liberal party's newspaper in Quebec
City, depicted Meighen mindlessly repeating "ready, aye
ready" while handing over a young Canadian soldier to
blood-stained hands labelled "Imperialism." Meighen was
called "the author of death," a war-crazed madman who,
upon election, would immediately conscript young men
and send them to their death. Meighen did not dignify
these ridiculous, unfair charges with a reply. That
Mackenzie King did not repudiate them is unfortunate
and to his lasting discredit. In any event, the campaign
in Quebec, however distasteful, was a successful one for
King: the Liberals won all but five of the province's
seats.

Elsewhere the 1925 election was more encouraging
for Meighen and his party. On October 30, 1925,
Meighen found himself leading the largest party in the
House, with 116 seats. The Progressives were reduced to
twenty seats; they had failed to gain the foothold in
Canadian politics which their sixty-five seats seemed to
promise in 1921. Their performance in the House was
not convincing, and they appeared to be little more than
Liberals in another dress. Many Progressive supporters
began to believe that their goals would be best achieved
if they worked from within the traditional parties rather
than challenging them from without. However, it was
still the Progressive bloc that denied the Conservatives a
majority.

Meighen especially savoured his personal victory in
Portage la Prairie, where he had suffered such embar-
rassment four years earlier and where some advisors had
warned him he had no chance in 1925. Discouragement
came only from Quebec and from Alberta where the
Tories won no seats. On the whole, the doubling of
Tory strength was an enormous achievement, a tribute
to Meighen's public performance and his private negotiations.

Characteristically, King was not ready to give up
although he had lost his majority. Refusing to resign, he
decided to meet Parliament. The decision was a shrewd
one, for within a few months the Conservatives were
once again fighting among themselves.

# Chapter 7 ... And Defeat

The spark which set off this renewed dissension was another Meighen speech. In Hamilton, Ontario, soon after the election, Meighen announced that if he were Prime Minister and war broke out, he would call an election to determine "the will of the people" before sending Canadian troops abroad. A harmless remark, it seems, but not to Canadian Tories in 1926. Had Meighen abandoned "ready, aye ready," changing position and principle like Mackenzie King? One Conservative newspaper thought he had: "While other parts of the Empire were fighting, Canadians would be voting. Bullets flying in the battle front and ballots flying in Canada."

In fact, hindsight suggests that Meighen's idea was a good one, but his timing was very bad. Perhaps an upcoming by-election in a French-Canadian riding explains why Meighen made his remarks. If so, they did not work; the Conservatives lost the by-election as well as some friends in English Canada. The most important loss, however, was in the momentum which the party had gained in the 1925 election. Now King's minority government had some time and freedom to manoeuvre and that, of course, King could do quite well.

When it came to wooing the Progressives, who held the balance of power in the House of Commons, Meighen was no match for King, the former labour arbitrator. Meighen's nature made concessions difficult; King's made them inevitable. Therefore, when the Progressives and the "Ginger Group" (a new left-wing group made up of labour politicians from Manitoba and agrarian radicals from Alberta and Ontario) asked the Liberal and Conservative leaders what they would offer in return for their support, they heard an echo of their own demands from King; from Meighen, only a reading of the Conservative platform. It came as no surprise when all but five Progressives sided with King against the Opposition amendment to the Speech from the Throne. It appeared that the King government might survive not just for months but for years.

*King in 1926*

Meighen was rescued from that fate by revelations made by his colleague Harry Stevens about the operation of the Customs Department. Stevens' first accusations led to the creation of a special committee to investigate his charges. What that committee uncovered probably astonished even Stevens. Smuggling, excise tax evasion and bribery were found throughout the department. Leading officials were leading smugglers as well, and there were hints that the Customs Minister himself was involved. In response to the report of the committee, King fired the Minister, Jacques Bureau, but then, in an astonishing move, he appointed him to the Senate. The Government's fall seemed likely when Stevens proposed a motion of censure of the government.

A providential angel for the government suddenly appeared in the surprising person of J.S. Woodsworth, the Winnipeg Socialist. Woodsworth was appalled by the corruption of the King government, and he realized that King's defeat would be richly deserved. Nevertheless, he also saw that the Parliamentary situation gave

*J.S. Woodsworth on Parliament Hill, 1923*

him an unusual degree of power: the power to destroy a government, the power to demand concessions. King was willing to make such concessions as the price of staying in power. It was a unique opportunity. Having decided that King's promise of old-age pensions was an end which justified questionable means, Woodsworth saved King by opposing the motion of censure.

The stormy debate which witnessed the bare survival

of the King government ended at five in the morning on Friday June 26, 1926. During the debate on the preceding evening, Mackenzie King, fearing that his government was doomed, had disappeared, his whereabouts unknown. He had, in fact, gone to ask the Governor General, Lord Byng, for a dissolution of the House of Commons. King thought he could probably survive an election on the issue, while without an election the House would surely hand the government to Meighen. Lord Byng, who was well aware of what was going on in the House, quite properly refused to go along. King's scheme was purely political, and Byng could not do anything which would favour one party over any other.

King, however, would not relent, insisting that the Governor General had no right to refuse his first minister's request for dissolution. Byng replied that "Mr. Meighen has not been given a chance of trying to govern or saying that he cannot do so, and that all reasonable expedients should be tried before resorting to another election." Faced with Byng's firm decision, King resigned on Monday, June 28, astonishing the House and the nation. Naturally, the Conservatives were exuberant — power was finally theirs. Meighen considered Byng's invitation to form a government and quickly accepted. This decision was a mistake.

Although it had been easy to accept the offer, Meighen found that forming a government under the circumstances presented unforeseen difficulties. He lacked a majority and had to depend upon the Progressives for support. Even worse, the law at the time required that any M.P. appointed to a cabinet portfolio had to resign and stand for election once again. This would almost certainly doom the Meighen government. Meighen therefore resorted to the unusual device of appointing ministers *without portfolio* who then became acting ministers of departments. The automatic resignations were avoided, but Meighen himself lost his seat when be became Prime Minister, so he was absent when his new government met the house.

The absence was unfortunate; without Meighen in the House, Mackenzie King attacked the constitutionality of the appointment of the ministers without portfolio. King's arguments were wrong, but neither the Conservatives nor the Progressives seemed to be paying attention

*Lord Byng*

*What functions do ministers without portfolio usually serve?*

to the arguments themselves. King was in top form. Seeing himself as a defender of the people's rights against autocratic methods and very much the grandson of William Lyon Mackenzie, the Liberal leader declared that Meighen's ministers were not accountable to Parliament and that Canada therefore lacked responsible government. This was the kind of language which impressed Progressives, and when the Liberals introduced a motion along these lines, the Progressives were perplexed. Should they support the new government as they had indicated earlier or should they register their objection to Meighen's "unconstitutional" methods? Most chose the latter course, and on July 2, 1926, the Meighen government was defeated, five days after it was formed. Canada faced another election.

Despite the debacle in the Commons, the Conservatives and Meighen remained confident. After all, had they not more than doubled their representation in 1925 and was not the Customs scandal still fresh in Canadian memories? Moreover, with Patenaude finally in the cabinet, Quebec seemed friendlier to the Conservatives than ever before. But the Conservatives were not allowed to fight the battle on friendly ground. Mackenzie King skilfully drew them into combat over what he termed the constitutional issue, the Governor General's refusal to grant him a dissolution. In short, King ran against Lord Byng, who was defenceless because of his office, rather than against Meighen.

*How has the role of the Governor General changed since Meighen's day? Could a constitutional crisis like the King-Byng affair recur today?*

It was a clever move indeed. King managed to make voters forget the Customs scandal. Instead, they were asked to reflect upon Canada's national status. Canadians in the 1920s were becoming nationalistic and coming to resent limitations upon Canadian sovereignty. King's charge that the Governor General had refused to follow the advice of his first minister, who had been elected by the Canadian people, aroused many Canadians. Meighen tried to show that the Governor General had acted correctly. His arguments may have convinced historians, but not Canadian voters in 1926.

On election day, the Conservatives fell back from their 1925 heights and King's Liberals advanced to capture the majority which had eluded Meighen a year earlier. Meighen once again lost his own seat, but unlike 1921, this time he knew he could not survive.

On September 26, 1926 Meighen resigned as Prime
Minister of Canada. Never again would his eloquent
words echo through the Commons, and for the next generation, King was spared Meighen's skilful oratory and
sharp sarcasm in daily debate. With his resignation, even
his opponents (Mackenzie King excepted) admitted his
abilities and recognized his remarkable career. *The
Manitoba Free Press*, for example, wrote: "To enter
Parliament at thirty-four, one of a horde of undistin-
guished raw recruits, and to become almost immediately
a parliamentary figure; to fight his way to the charmed
government ranks in six years; to win premiership at
forty-six, to attain and hold against all comers the
position of the first swordsman of Parliament — these
are achievements which will survive the disaster of
today." The epitaph was premature. Meighen's sword
was sheathed but was never allowed to dull. It would
join another fight at a later day.

# Chapter 8 Quiet Years

Meighen left politics with few regrets but with some bitterness. He had achieved so much, but it seemed to him and his friends that his talent and ambition should have brought him even farther. That Mackenzie King had grasped the ring of power so securely was especially annoying to Meighen, but to remain in politics just to annoy King could only be done at considerable loss to his own dignity and self-esteem. At the age of fifty-two, Arthur Meighen therefore began a search for a new career. The former prime minister was not unemployed for long.

Business had always attracted Meighen, as his disastrous venture in dried fruit reveals. When a friend asked him to join him in an enterprising investment firm, Meighen eagerly agreed. The stock market during the boom of the 1920s proved much kinder to Meighen than either dried fruit or politics had been. His own financial worth multiplied rapidly, and he felt comfortable and confident with his new colleagues on Toronto's Bay Street. One unfortunate sign of his new prosperity and his less strenuous life was a rather portly appearance. No longer could journalists compare Meighen to Shakespeare's "lean and hungry" Cassius. But despite his new relaxed appearance the old intensity remained in many ways.

One of Meighen's new friends, the distinguished Canadian poet and Professor of English Literature at the University of Toronto, E.J. Pratt, testified to Meighen's extraordinary dedication which he encountered on their first meeting at the golf course:

Mr. Meighen came up to the first tee without a golf bag but he had one club in his hand — a putter. And I saw the strangest sight, a man hitting from a tee with a putter. He used only the putter all through the course. I thought to myself, 'His score will be about two hundred.' But the amazing thing was what he did with it. He always drove dead down the middle of the fairway, about 130 yards indeed, but even that was incredible. When he came within range of the pin he became more deliberate and cautious; the crowd behind yelling 'Fore!' didn't disturb him. He would take a parliamentary stance and by some kind of calculus known only to himself he would assess all the factors and then he would strike. The pin was up there like a political opponent which had to be outmanoeuvred, not so much reached as attacked.

Pratt overcame his astonishment and became a good friend. For his part, Meighen thought little of Pratt's often complex poetry, but he admired Pratt's knowledge of English literature. He and Pratt spend many hours discussing Shakespeare, "the greatest Englishman of them all," as Meighen once called him. Others besides Pratt discovered that the politician who seemed so narrow was a man with broad interests and knowledge and a fund of anecdotes; in short, he was good company. His closest friends were often not Conservatives; indeed, one of the closest, Eugene Forsey, was a socialist and a frequent (although unsuccessful) socialist candidate for Parliament. The partisan who had aroused such hatred among his enemies proved to be a delightful companion even among Liberals and socialists when he moved outside the political arena.

Despite Meighen's own good intentions, his absence from political involvement was brief. It was not any friendship with his successor as Conservative leader, R.B. Bennett that brought him back to politics, however. He and Bennett were Western rivals who had quarrelled

*Meighen and R.B. Bennett in 1938*

publicly and bitterly. Since his election as leader in 1927, Bennett had studiously ignored Meighen. But Meighen had too many friends and commanded too much respect among Conservatives to be allowed to remain in exile in Toronto when the Conservatives gained power in Ottawa in 1930.

Politics no doubt seemed attractive again to Meighen, for it was through political leadership that the Great Depression, which had begun in 1929, would have to be solved. The Depression had also dulled the lustre and attractiveness of Meighen's business career, and had given him some anxiety when he thought of the decline in his personal wealth and, even worse, in the funds he managed for friends, admirers and clients. Meighen was therefore prepared to leave Toronto in 1932 when Bennett offered him a Senate appointment and a cabinet position as Government Leader in the Senate. Meighen, like so many other House of Commons titans, was reluctant to enter the Upper Chamber, whose galleries were mostly empty and whose debates were invariably ignored. Yet the offer was a generous one: he could continue his business career in Toronto, coming to Ottawa only during the session and attending Cabinet only when he chose.

*Critics of the Senate complain that it is used only to reward party members for services such as campaign contributions. Or it can become a haven for those such as Jacques Bureau, King's Minister of Customs. What was the original purpose of the Senate? Does it still serve that purpose?*

Thus at the rather early age of fifty-eight Meighen became an elder statesman, above the rough-and-tumble of politics but still close enough to the battle to advise the combatants and prevent calamities. It was a comfortable stance; Meighen and Bennett would not have been able to tolerate each other at closer range. Moreover, Meighen had no more worthwhile proposals for solutions to the mass unemployment, poverty and despair of the Depression than Bennett. He had become too much of a businessman and was inclined to reflect the business world's conservative approach to social change and social welfare. In times of distress, a businessman could cut costs; why shouldn't government do the same? That, of course, was exactly what the government should not have done in the 1930s because indiscriminate cost-cutting only exaggerated the impact of the Depression. Meighen did not oppose limited state assistance to ease the effect of mass unemployment, but he deeply feared extensive state involvement in the economy along the lines of Franklin Roosevelt's policies in the United States

at this time. He believed such state intervention would diminish self-reliance, thrift, and individual initiative, the qualities he cherished so much. Perhaps it was just as well that Meighen stayed on the sidelines while the politicians of the 1930s struggled to escape from under the debris of economic collapse.

Meighen found his political beliefs as well as his economic ones challenged in the 1930s. The new wave was populism, and Meighen, who had come to belittle the wisdom of the average man, felt it was a dangerous trend.

One of the great Canadian populists was William "Bible Bill" Aberhart, who started the Social Credit movement in the West. Much of his influence was gained by the sheer force of his rhetoric. He started

*Unemployed men board a train in Alberta to join in protest march on Ottawa, June 1935*

*The term populism has been applied to many political movements. What are its characteristics?*

public life as a radio preacher, and when he entered politics, he was the first Canadian to use radio extensively for political campaigning. His talent for speech-making thus used to maximum advantage, he gained a wide following among prairie farmers and eventually became Premier of Alberta.

Ontario's best-known populist was Mitch Hepburn, an onion farmer who entered the Ontario legislature as a Liberal in 1926. Hepburn once gave this neat description of his ideology: "The little guy does not get enough of the good things of life, and anyway it's good politics to give a hand to the majority." Like Aberhart, Hepburn was a lively orator. He was a rough and often dirty politician who enjoyed getting his political enemies into trouble. One of those he chose to annoy was Arthur Meighen.

Meighen had been serving on Ontario's Hydro-Electric Power Commission since 1931. In the spring of 1933, Hepburn began making charges against Meighen and Conservative Premier George Henry. Meighen was accused of securing excessively large power contracts for a company in which he and Henry held stock. The company went bankrupt and the province had to buy it out. When he became Premier in 1934, Hepburn set up a Royal Commission to investigate the affair, but Meighen felt it was not a fair one. He complained: "This is the

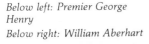

*Below left: Premier George Henry*
*Below right: William Aberhart*

most diabolical political inquisition ever held outside of Turkey. The conduct of it would put to shame Pontius Pilate."

Meighen was right about the inquiry. The commission's final report ignored sworn testimony in Meighen's defence, and the whole business looked very much like a fishing expedition. The truth of the matter was that

*Mitchell Hepburn*

*Robert J. Manion*

*The King government was embarrassed in 1932 by Meighen's persistence in investigating the involvement of three Liberal Senators in government power contracts with the Beauharnois company.*

Meighen had only an indirect interest in the company and little or no influence in awarding power contracts. Although he had been in the right, Meighen felt his personal honour had been insulted by the charges of corruption. It seemed to him that he was being harassed by the Liberals for having criticized them in 1932, when the Liberals had gotten into trouble in the Beauharnois affair.

The Hepburn "inquisition" certainly did not soften Meighen's attitude toward Hepburn personally or toward politics in general in the 1930s. As a Conservative and a businessman, he felt keenly the sting of populist attacks on party machines and big business. The victory of the "little man" would destroy the traditions from which Meighen had come.

If Meighen was increasingly distrustful of the direction of Canadian politics, he nevertheless remained deeply involved in it as Leader of the Conservatives in the Senate. Bennett, who had become even more disillusioned than Meighen, was defeated in 1935 by King, and a few years later he left politics and Canada to join the British nobility. His successor as Conservative leader, Robert Manion, was a pleasant, intelligent, and humane politician, but he was neither Meighen's choice nor Bennett's equal. Meighen believed that Manion was too liberal, too willing to bring in "socialist" schemes disguised by Conservative window-dressing. There was an even deeper disagreement between the two men on what Canada should do if a war came: would there be conscription and a fight "to the last man and the last dollar" as in World War I? In normal times, this difference of opinion would matter little, but after 1938 normal times were slipping away quickly, as war became a real possibility.

Canada did not want to become involved in another European war; the last one had cost far too much. Yet by 1939 most Canadian had become convinced that Hitler's Germany, like Kaiser Wilhelm's, was an evil force which could threaten all of Western civilization. When German armour and air power swept across Poland in September 1939, Britain and France decided to act to halt the aggressor. A few days later Canada joined the Allied cause. There was little protest but much nervous apprehension, for neither Canada's politicians nor her people had any idea what the cost of the war would be.

Mackenzie King vowed that there would be no repetition of the French-English clash of World War I. He promised immediately and publicly that his government would never impose conscription. This seemed to Meighen a foolish promise, but one that he had expected from King. However, when Manion made the same promise, Meighen was simply outraged and became further convinced that Manion was a weak and inadequate leader. He would have to leave, against his own will if necessary.

Meighen, with the memory of the 1917 coalition strong in his mind, promoted the cause of National Government, a government composed not of a single party but of the "best" men in the nation. Naturally, he thought that he and his friends would be counted among the best. In such a government the pygmies, Manion and King, would inevitably fade into the background as the strong men took over. But Meighen's plan was never tried: Liberals would not desert King and they had no desire to include Conservatives in their government. When King called a surprise election in 1940, his supporters rallied about him. The Liberal campaign in that election was so effective that they trounced the Conservatives in both English and French Canada and thereby brought the National Government movement to an abrupt halt. Manion, understandably exasperated at his party's disunity and frustrated by the Liberal triumph, resigned. Once again Conservative eyes turned towards Arthur Meighen.

# Second Chance Chapter 9

Meighen did not shun the new attention; indeed, he seemed to encourage it. Consider Meighen's position: he had left the centre of the political stage fifteen years ago. During his exile, he had been a prophet in the wilderness, warning Canadians that they could not close their eyes to events in Europe. Like that other great political outsider, Winston Churchill, he had told his countrymen what they did not want to hear — now they knew they must listen. On May 10, 1940, as the British war effort faltered, Churchill became Britain's prime minister and immediately revitalized his nation's outlook. On that evening Churchill slept soundly for the first time since the war began, confident that the government was in good hands. Similarly, Meighen could not rest until Canada's war effort was in safe hands. But unlike Churchill, Meighen did not crave the prime minister's position. He merely wanted enough power to put Canada on a proper wartime course.

Meighen's desire to play a leading part was intensified after the Liberal victory in 1940. Despite King's reassurances, the war was going very badly, both in Europe and at home. There was evidence of disorganization in Ottawa, but far more serious was the invasion threat facing Britain after the fall of France in the early summer of 1940. Dunkirk, the evacuation of 250 000 British soldiers from France, photographs of London burning and tales of Nazi brutality rekindled pro-British sentiments in English-Canadian hearts, and throughout English Canada there arose a call for a greater war effort.

Meighen, of course, shared these concerns and expressed them at the Conservative convention in November 1941. The delegates were delighted; here was the man to defeat the faint-hearted Mackenzie King. The convention passed a resolution asking Arthur Meighen to accept the leadership. That night Meighen considered his future and, more important, his past. By dawn he knew he could not accept.

The vote on the resolution had been 37 for, 13

*How were party leaders chosen before conventions?*

against; and the nays had a case which Meighen had to acknowledge. When asked to state his answer to the convention's request, Meighen declared:

Those 13 men doubtless represent many throughout the country and among them doubtless are men without whose ardent support, without any reservation in the world in their hearts and their minds, I wouldn't dream of accepting this terrible responsibility. I therefore shall not.

The words must have come with great difficulty, but Meighen knew he had to say them. He wanted power, and he knew that at sixty-seven years of age it was his last chance. Yet the images from the past — the conscription debate, the famous cartoon where his hands dripped with blood, and most of all, the scorn of French Canadians whenever they uttered Meighen's name — all these images and more went through his mind and warned him to resist the persuasive tactics planned by the convention.

Meighen knew best, but his friends would not give up. His telephone rang continuously. "For the sake of the party, accept," the callers pleaded in desperate voices. Eventually, Meighen gave in, agreeing to become Conservative leader on the platform of 1917: a coalition government that would bring in conscription. He resigned from the Senate and prepared to enter the House of Commons in a by-election in South York (Toronto) which was called for February 9, 1942. He expected that a victorious campaign in a Conservative, English-Canadian riding such as South York would provide the spearhead for a determined national effort to bring down Mackenzie King. This vision gained substance when the Liberals, following the custom of not opposing new opposition leaders in by-elections, declined to nominate a candidate. The C.C.F. was not so obliging, but their candidate, Joseph Noseworthy, had trailed in a field of three in the last South York election and he seemed to present no threat. The path was clear.

Within a few weeks however, obstacles appeared and, as in the past, Meighen showed a determination to run them over rather than gracefully elude them. Very few voters in South York were socialists, the natural supporters of Noseworthy, and Meighen could have exploited this fact by drawing the lines between socialism and free enterprise. He foolishly failed to do so. Instead Meighen concentrated his attack upon Mackenzie King

*Joseph Noseworthy*

and the Liberals, virtually ignoring Noseworthy. He hammered the government on its refusal to conscript, its lacklustre war leadership, and its refusal to form a National Government. Meighen's speeches received national attention, and his triumphant return was expected by all — all, that is, except Joseph Noseworthy and his friends.

Noseworthy wisely refused to be drawn into the verbal battle between Meighen and the Liberals. Instead he and his supporters walked from street to street, house to house, knocking on door after door. His major appeal was not to the C.C.F. supporters but rather to the riding's many Liberals, who were increasingly offended by Meighen's biting remarks about the party and the leader whom they traditionally supported. Meighen, the C.C.F. charged, had not changed; he was still the narrow-minded servant of the Bay Street interests who had little knowledge of and no sympathy for the "common man." Meighen would conscript workers but not the wealth of their employers. It was a very effective tactic, and Meighen's failure to reply to the C.C.F. hurt him badly.

Another serious blow to Meighen's chances was administered in the middle of the campaign by Meighen's old adversary, Mackenzie King. Seeing that his pledge not to impose conscription was becoming unpopular, King announced a plebiscite to determine whether Canadians would free him from the pledge. With this move, King deftly muffled the conscription issue in the South York campaign. After all, why should conscriptionists become involved in the South York campaign when they could vote on the question itself in a few months? Meighen was furious. Surely this was only another example of King's slipperiness and dishonesty. But Meighen's angry words only served to convince many

*Conscription supporters with a Rooney Club dog cart, 1942*

Liberals that they must keep him out of Parliament; and on February 9, they did.

Meighen suffered the most embarrassing defeat of his career as Noseworthy won by a large margin. Both King and Meighen knew that never again would Meighen dare to challenge King's political power. Indeed, King, who had believed that Meighen would win, thought that God had intervened in human affairs to keep Meighen out of the House of Commons. With Meighen's defeat, King wrote in his diary, "public life in Canada had been cleansed" of a force which was "truly vile or bad." But if King was a graceless winner, Meighen was a poor loser. He failed to see that his own campaign tactics rather than Liberal trickery had produced his defeat. He blamed the voters' ignorance, not his own.

For Meighen, there remained only the task of finding a successor, and he did not look long. John Bracken, Liberal-Progressive Premier of Manitoba, was Meighen's choice. Earlier, before he had accepted the leadership himself, Meighen had tried unsuccessfully to persuade Bracken to give up the premier's office for that of Leader of the Opposition. Now he called again on Bracken in Manitoba to persuade him of how important it was that Mackenzie King be beaten. The fact that Bracken was not a Conservative does not seem to have troubled Meighen. It was important that the Conservatives acquire a popular leader who had a reputation for effi-ciency and honesty. Bracken, however, knew that many Conservatives would be very unhappy if an outsider took over their leadership. Consequently, he refused to give Meighen any commitment before the convention, which was called for December in Winnipeg.

Not knowing what would follow, Meighen, defeated but defiant, spoke on opening day. It was a valedictory address but it lacked the few kind words for opponents which are normally included on such occasions. Macken-zie King, Meighen claimed, did not dare to tell the truth. King's party was the "heir of its discreditable past," en-tangled in "the meshes of a sorry history." But now others would have to lead the fight against this evil gov-ernment. Thirty-five years — more than a generation — after the modest farmers and businessmen of Portage la Prairie first nominated him, Meighen bluntly said good-bye: "Gentlemen, I am through." Characteristically, he

*John Bracken*

refused to go quietly into the political night. In a stirring conclusion, Meighen summarized his career and outlook:

Fortune came and fortune fled; believe in my sincerity when I say that this is no reason for sympathy. It is only the lot of all of us, at least of all who strive — the joy of the upward struggle, the successes, disappointments and defeats. Perhaps it has been my fate to have had more than the average on both sides of the account, but I promise you there is going to be nothing of bitterness carried forward after the page is turned. As a matter of truth, health and happiness have been better in adversity and no man need feel that he has failed unless, in looking back, the retrospect is blank, or unless time and events have proved that he was wrong. Whether now judged right or wrong, whatever I have said, whatever I have done, is going to remain unrevised and unrepented. As it is, it will await whatever verdict may come. The future can assess it or forget it, and it will be all right with me.

Shortly thereafter the convention chose Meighen's man Bracken. Despite his promise, it was not "all right" with Meighen after 1942. So long as Mackenzie King ruled, Meighen could not be content, and King remained for six more years. Bracken was defeated in 1945, and he too abandoned the leadership of a party which seemed almost impossible to lead. Meighen was disappointed but not surprised. The result of universal suffrage appeared to be irresponsibility both on the part of the electorate and of the elected. Politicians purchased votes through "bribes" — welfare schemes which only dulled the initiative and energy of the workers. Family allowances, which King had introduced in time for the election of 1945, were an example of the attractiveness and also of the danger of such schemes. From such small beginnings, the state would extend its web over all aspects of private life. Eventually, individual freedom would suffocate beneath the overwhelming burden of a charity state.

It was a bleak picture that Meighen envisaged, to be sure, but not one which he allowed to affect his private enjoyment. He had turned seventy years old in 1944, and he knew that every future year depended upon God's good grace. He cherished every moment, especially those spent with his family and friends. His wife "Nan" remained sprightly, a constant and valuable companion. His children, now adults, had become successful. Max had joined his father in Canadian General Securities, which prospered greatly in the post-war boom — a boom for which Meighen gave Mackenzie King no credit. As Max took over his father's work, Meighen found more time for old friends. The range of his friendships remained very wide, and his supply of anecdotes apparently limitless. He refought the battles of the past; now, of course, he won many of them, at least in the eyes of his friends.

Meighen's strong constitution, which was hidden behind a frail appearance, carried him into his ninth decade. He lived to see the election of another Conservative government in 1957, but his faculties were failing and the times were different; no longer could he relish the victory as he would have years before. On August 4, 1960, Arthur Meighen died in his sleep in Toronto. Three days later, his body was brought back to St. Mary's.

On that August afternoon in Meighen's home town, there were few people who recalled the shy, diligent bookworm of St. Mary's Collegiate Institute. Most remembered the man of politics, and many must have

found it puzzling that the quiet slopes and valleys around them could have brought forth the angry, controversial public figure they knew so well. And yet Meighen's career can best be understood through his birthplace and his early years. Meighen was born into a society very much different from that of the larger community which he felt called upon to lead. First St. Mary's and then Portage la Prairie had presented him with communities whose limits were clearly visible. Each had within it a system, a hierarchy, where everyone found his place easily. The patterns of life were clear: one knew the past and, in most cases, the future. The bright, future leader and the laggard could be identified from their first days in the village school, and rarely were the predictions wrong.

In those debates in the collegiate where Meighen excelled, he always knew he could argue either side because everyone around him shared certain basic assumptions about man and society. In his party and with his friends, Meighen continued to find this certainty throughout his life. He knew his own world so well he failed to understand there was another. For all his ambition, energy, and talent, he never climbed the mountain to see beyond to the other side.

## Further Reading

Brown, R.C. and Cook, Ramsay. *Canada 1896-1921: A Nation Transformed.* McClelland & Stewart, Toronto, 1974.

Graham, Roger. *Arthur Meighen,* 3 vols. Clarke, Irwin, Toronto, 1960-65. A sympathetic biography, approved by Meighen.

Granatstein, J.L. *The Politics of Survival: The Conservative Party of Canada, 1939-1945.* University of Toronto Press, Toronto, 1976.

Macbeth, Madge. *The Land of Afternoon.* Graphic Publishers, Ottawa, 1924. A satire on the Ottawa scene; the Prime Minister is modelled on Meighen.

Meighen, Arthur. *The Greatest Englishman of History.* Oxford University Press, Toronto, 1936. An address on Shakespeare.

_____. *Unrevised and Unrepented: Debating Speeches and Others.* Clarke, Irwin, Toronto, 1949.

---

## Credits

*Editing:* Barbara Czarnecki
*Design:* Jack Steiner
*Cover Illustration:* Leoung O'Young

**The Canadians**

*Consulting Editor:* Roderick Stewart
*Editor-in-Chief:* Robert Read

Every effort has been made to credit all sources correctly. The author and publishers will welcome any information that will allow them to correct any errors or omissions.